Advance praise for Wildfire: Poems for Our Planet

Two inspiring poets, Cath Davies and Lisa Rossetti. Two people who care about people. Care about the survival of our planet, and the huge challenges we all have to care about. Both writers touch the very heart of these subjects.

"Letter To A Nuclear World" by Cath Davies or "War Drums" by Lisa Rossetti. "Warming Woman" by Cath Davies. "Minerva's Shrine," by Lisa Rossetti. But I will say no more. Pick this book up and read it!

Maureen Weldon, Poet & Former Professional Ballet Dancer

This collection of poems is organised as a challenge, a stark call to action in facing the realities of life viewed through the lens of: the victim, the silenced, forgotten, overlooked, absent, eroded, destroyed, memories, dreams, nightmares, life, and death. These poems bring the eye and focus to pay attention to those quieter voices, to vocalise their experiences and honour them in a non-sentimental clear and direct way.

They are honest, refreshing, offering the reader a kind of truth, facing what is rather than avoiding, uncovering what is often pushed away as unpleasant fact.

This is what the news would be like if presented in poetry. It bears witness to how the world news impacts each and every one of us, and how simple rituals of our everyday lives ground us like the soil at our feet, reminding us of hope in the words of the poem 'All is to be dared'.

Dawn McHale, Poet & Storyteller

This collection is urgent and raw. It is difficult to imagine that the issues explored will only become more urgent, unless we manage to address the concerns that the poems highlight.

The authors have ably and articulately exposed the frailties of our global lives, and how cultural blindness will limit solutions. This is an important collection.

Deborah Humphrey, Creative Writing Practitioner

I read the poems and was totally overwhelmed with how powerful they are.

Karen Harvey, Poet

Wildfire

Poems for Our Planet

Lisa Rossetti & Cath Davies

Published in Great Britain in 2024

Copyright © Lisa Rossetti & Cath Davies 2024

Cover design copyright © Ceri York
at 24 Steps Art & Design 2024

All rights reserved. No part of this publication may be reproduced, distributed or transmitted in any form or by any means, including photocopying, recording, or other electronic or mechanical methods, without the prior written permission of the publisher.

ISBN: 9798872363361

Contents

War — *11 - 20*

- Pages — 12
- Waving — 13
- Freshly Cut Grass — 14
- Global Sacrifice — 15
- Brink — 16
- Letter To A Nuclear World — 17
- In The Dark — 18
- Indelible — 20

Politics — *21 - 25*

- Twenty Twenty Two — 22
- Poem To A Lost Queen — 23
- Remembering The Poem — 24
- Grenfell Tower — 25

Poverty — *27 - 31*

- War Drums — 28
- Why? — 29
- A Lift To All Floors — 30
- But All Is To Be Dared — 31

Homelessness — *32 - 36*

- Josie's Room — 33
- Difference — 34
- Roof — 35
- Housewife 49 Revisited — 36

Mental Health — *37 - 42*

- Bitter Wind — 38
- Film With No Star — 39
- Sand Dog — 40
- How Jimmy Died — 41
- Shit Into Compost — 42

Climate *43 - 49*

- Warming Woman — 44
- Listening To The Grasslands — 45
- Wildfire — 46
- Climate Conference — 47
- Generation Zero — 48
- Compartments — 49

History and Place *50 - 54*

- Chester's Child Soldiers — 51
- The Birds Can Read — 52
- Liverpool One — 53
- Minerva's Shrine — 54

Affirmation and Hope *55 - 67*

- Life Calls — 56
- Tight In The Bud — 57
- Redemption Rain — 58
- The Wrong Number — 60
- We Stand For Life — 61
- Basic Rules For Nighttime Spellcasting — 63
- Sashiko For The Soul — 65
- Sentences — 66
- Young Hearts — 67

Acknowledgements *68*

About The Authors *69*

*To climate activists everywhere –
keep telling truth to power*

Cath

*To all staff and volunteers at Networks for Nature and
Wildlife Connections at Chester Zoo –
for everything you do to nurture wildlife*

Lisa

War

Pages

Today is a page of history.

If you read it yesterday,
you would not
read it as a prayer book.

But it is.

Cath Davies

Waving

This was their house.
The washing line waves its bright colours aloft:
A small girl's lilac frock
patterned with pretty summer flowers,
Grandmother's shawl,
a father's honest work shirt,
a sheet, a towel.
Dancing together in the breeze.
The breeze lifts a small cloud of dust
from the shattered bricks,
the gaping hole in the wall.
Their bodies lie under the stones.

Lisa Rossetti

Freshly Cut Grass

You come in from the garden,
freshly cut grass tramping in with you.

You have marshalled leaves,
and dragged creosote down the fence.

You have ruptured weeds,
and run fingers under a warm tap.

Then you turn on the news.
I look outside the window in horror.

Cath Davies

Global Sacrifice

The sky is full of blood;
the moon a dirty fingernail.
We hear the roar of the Wolf,
hide our children in the dark –
we cannot find the magic
to save them from the madness.
Horror eclipses our lives;
in the cauldron of Hecate
our flesh melts like silver.

Lisa Rossetti

Brink

Please talk, politicians,
generals, murderers.
For I like to think
my lips mouthed words
before the fire.
The atom split,
and my hopes vapourised.
It took my body.
Obliterated all else.
And now I am spirit,
sending down feathers
to a burning world
that is made for talking
and lovers.

Cath Davies

Letter To A Nuclear World

Winter descends.
To the limits of imagination,
armageddon is a memory;
a grimace of God.
I have died from radiation sickness,
and my soul walks streets
littered with ash.
Ghosts ascend; I was never religious,
but I believed.
In peace. Equality.
I was Western, and in an ended world.
No warnings came.
The holocaust set light
to the atmosphere,
and only dreams were left.
Through them,
I live again.
The way wildlife
creeps down broken streets
but no people crowd in.
In Heaven, I give warnings to angels
with no ears; peace
is nothing unless on Earth.
Everybody fights,
but in a nuclear world,
nobody can afford to.

Cath Davies

In The Dark

It is dark. I stand at the back of the school hall in my red coat,
craning my neck to look over the silhouettes of mums and dads.
On the stage, the children's faces are brightly lit;
I search for my grandson.
We all sway together to the familiar sounds
of Christmas celebration: Silent Night, Holy Night.

The mother crouches in the dark. She cannot
find her children. They are lost
somewhere in the shattered city, in Aleppo.
It is another fearful night; a desperate scene
lit with faux fireworks.

On the stage, the prettiest girls swirl and twirl in silver dresses.
They are Snowflakes. The ungainly ones totter around
dressed as clumsy stars. A geeky boy in specs is trying
to clap in time to the music. You can almost hear him
counting under his breath, one, two, three – one, two, three.

Dust clouds swirl about her like snow.
The bombers come again, that familiar sound.
She counts them flying overhead,
carrying their deathly cargo – one, two, three.
Their black bellies blot out the stars.

The lights come on again; the spell of the play is broken.
I can still see Mary cradling the doll child;

and Joseph standing by in the customary nightgown
and tea towel headgear, leaning on his staff.

A Christmas card scene; a family seeks shelter.
Through the streets of Aleppo, fathers carry
their newborn in their arms.
They walk towards us again and again,
in prayer, in hope, in despair.
This time, will the ceasefire hold?

The children gather in the corridor, waiting for their parents.
They hitch up the awkward robes, remove the tottering crowns.
They will go home to their stripey pyjamas and Ovaltine,
then early to bed to dream of golden kings,
silvery snowflakes and dancing mice.

Fatima walks beside her father in her scarlet boots;
They take their place in the long silent line.
Tonight in the camp, her head will be filled with unquiet dreams.
She will cry for the mother and brothers, all dead.
The kings of the world play with their lives.

Tomorrow in class, the boys will josh each other and jeer:
'You forgot your lines', 'You farted!', 'You were rubbish!'
The prettiest girls will preen and pose, with one more twirl
and the ungainly Stars will feel left out once more.
The geeky boy will push his specs up his nose.

At home I switch on the Six o'clock News, hoping
it might all be different. For one night we hoped
the Christmas magic was real. Tonight I pray aloud
that all God's children will rule the world,
and free us from our bad dreams.

Lisa Rossetti

Indelible
for Gaza's innocent children*

When darkness fell
bringing more fires,
the children cried,
 "Write our names!"
We grabbed our black Sharpies
And wrote on their bare legs -
Amal, Nasreen, Samira, Ismail.
In the morning we covered them,
growing cold.

*Children in Gaza ask for their names to be written on their hands or legs so they will be recognised in the rubble.

Lisa Rossetti

Politics

Twenty Twenty Two

A year. A tsunami.
An uncoupling
of our collective health,
our lungs and mind.
Our workplaces set adrift
to dock at home.
And in all this, technology rises
like a monolith
with no clear edges.
No point in space but is our space.
We kneel for it,
spirituality in flux.
A companion that walks with us
yet changes direction.
And I hope.
I go on hoping.
For the eight billion of us
that are still human.
Half animal,
half artificial mind.
Thinking through our devices,
our hearts yet left behind.

Cath Davies

Poem To A Lost Queen

Today, the day after,
a union jack
still hangs from my neighbour's window.
The Daily Mail
has a whole edition to yesterday,
and social media
shares itself to millions.

I walk to work,
sadder than anyone can see,
and pass a postbox
out of date,
containing letters with stamps
also out of date.
Everything, out of date.

For my long years
I sang without thinking
God Save The Queen.
And now I will sing the same
but to the King.
And one day, I won't sing anything.
Life is like that.

Cath Davies

Remembering The Poem

Before she remembered the poem,
the world was white noise.

A mix of multiple frequencies,
crossed wires,
programmes concluding for no reason,
delayed announcements,
a mountain of information,
cancellations,
and a nonsense channel.

But after she remembered the poem,
the world was in tune again.

It was like a forgotten muse
had caught her attention in the static.

Cath Davies

Grenfell Tower

16th June, 2017

Those stairs'll be the death of me,
Her mother pants as she hauls the pushchair
up the final steps to her daughter's flat.

Why can't they fix the bloody lifts? Get it sorted?
She shrugs. *Nothing works round here, Mum. We keep telling 'em.
Yeah,* she sighs. *They don't listen. Well, I'll see you tomorrow, ok?*

She watches her mother slowly disappear,
trudging up the gloomy stairwell.
She calls out after her, *Lights not working again?*

In her kitchen she tips cornflakes into his Batman bowl,
grabs some cat food from the fridge. The light flickers inside
on and off, on and off. She kicks the fridge door shut.

Scooping up his cereal he shouts, *Sing me the song, Mum!*
He learnt a new one today at nursery – such a clever boy!
And handsome, they say to her. *Sure to break a few hearts!*

She pulls him onto her knee in his Superman pyjamas.
They both sing the familiar rhyme – *London's burning!
London's burning!*
He claps his sticky hands – *Fetch the engines! Fetch the engines!*

She carries him to the window in her arms
to look at the lights scattered across the city at night,
shining like jewels in a vast treasure chest.

Swallows circle the Tower, skimming
through the soft summer skies.
Soon the sun will set like a fireball.

Far below, a boy in a red hoodie
kicks a football in and out
of the concrete bollards.

In the night, she hears him cough,
but she's knackered and turns over,
completely dead to the world.
*   *   *
Firefighters find them in the morning,
Huddled together under the blown out window.

A cat's skull lies close by, and a blackened toy;
just a blob of plastic, stuck to what was once a small hand.
*   *   *
The onus for Fire and Safety provision should lie with the fire service; not with the Government.
Furthermore, we do not believe water sprinklers may be the best method of putting out fires.

In his parliamentary office, the Minister casually flicks up and
down his smartphone's screen.
His property market portfolio is doing very well, he notes.
He reaches for his brandy.

Lisa Rossetti

Poverty

War Drums

The drums are drumming.
A reckoning is coming.

In the creche the children play
with coloured beads.
One toddler tries out his words;
here's Red and Blue and Green.

His mother is spruced up
in black boots and white trousers,
hair piled high above a pallid face,
lines etched into her forehead.

I bring her coffee and cake;
it's free for food bank users.
She's waiting for her partner.
She doesn't want to talk.

He's out there fending for his family,
doing his best. He's tracking down
that vital red voucher,
somewhere in this city.

Two plastic bags will hold
three days' emergency rations.
We throw in some treats for the kids.
Vouchers and rations? What kind of war is this?

Lisa Rossetti

Why?

His eye is half closed,
scar tissue bunched together as if
a sword blow had struck him
right across the face.

He rises to leave
with his two little bags of food.
His right side is weak.
He struggles to carry them.

I've never had a proper job, he says.
Just been sent on those schemes, Remploy.
But I had to care for my wife –
she was in a wheelchair.

I don't ask if they're separated,
maybe she's dead. None of my business.

I told them when they did my assessment,
I can't go out anymore.
Well, how could I afford it?
I just sit on the sofa on my own.

And the assessor asked him,
Why haven't you killed yourself yet?

Lisa Rossetti

A Lift To All Floors

The lift is mobility,
a classless UK,
where we can aspire
to be the things you say.

The lift is equality,
you have run out of ideas
if you lie to us
and ignite our fears.

The lift is diversity,
the trouble you take
to give us the information
so we stay awake.

The lift is the word,
the floor is literature,
a sliding door
of success, not failure.

The lift is metaphor,
we give it your love,
so it reaches every level,
not just yours above.

Cath Davies

But All Is To Be Dared

But all is to be dared,
because even a person of poverty
has a fire burning in their heart,
though their hearth may seem bare and cold.
I could almost say the fire in the heart is vast,
though the embers are barely visible,
banked over with worries and cares,
the numbing of the daily grind.
No play of light on water,
no toes in warm white sand.
Crumbs instead of feasts.
Silverfish run up the walls,
cockroaches lurk in shadows.
The carpet is a map of grime.
Snails in the kitchen
eating the cats' meat.
Shame at the school gate,
the kids' shoes are down at heel.
Grubby sleeves unravel.
How can the fire be ignited
when all is to be dared,
but we dare not, we dare not?

Lisa Rossetti

Homelessness

Josie's Room

Josie's small room has an al fresco view
plenty of fresh air
She's not in when I call to say hello
sorry to miss her
she's left her bag in the entrance
with her drawing pad (she's an artist)
she's been doing some housekeeping
a dustpan and brush are propped against the wall
she's left her pair of pink trainers
beside her bed, slightly awry
she's carefully folded her duvet
it's a bit grubby but then you cannot fit
a washing machine into a doorway
I straighten her trainers neatly.

Lisa Rossetti

Difference

They were a nuisance, everyone agreed.
No better than vermin.
Cluttering up the city centre.
An eyesore. Filthy.

They hadn't much to call a home,
just a dirty doorway, an abandoned shop.
The Council received several angry petitions.
Drive them out, they said. It's not safe.

The way they look at you
with those nasty greedy eyes,
ready to snatch at anything.
Bad for tourism.

Nets didn't work.
Their numbers grew.
Still they huddled together,
muttering who knows what.

One winter's morning,
when they fluttered down
I had nothing in my pockets.
A few crumbs would have made all the difference.

Lisa Rossetti

Roof

Never gave a toss for what they thought of him in school.
He was bounced from pillar to crumbling post.
They say I've got complex problems, whatever the fuck that is.

Started out on the grown-ups' sherry, went on to weed and smack.
Getting drunk was a laugh, and robbing houses was fun, he said.
Got caught, let out, went back to the streets.
Gonna get a fucking bag.

He sleeps in a wheelie bin now. It's dry at least.
They asked, *Has it got a lid on it?* and laughed.
Well, you're not homeless, 'cos you've got a roof over your head!

Lisa Rossetti

Housewife 49 Revisited

It's busy in the community kitchen tonight;
a battalion of volunteers bustles about.
How would Housewife 49 have fared here,
in her headscarf and flowered pinnie?

She'd understand the battle,
this urgency to care for lost souls
battling through cruel, dark times.

She'd recognise our apple pie and custard
served up in thick china bowls.
It's the spirit of the Blitz.

Would she find it strange to see men in aprons
or serving out the tea? Just like her,
we make it strong, with plenty of sugar.

There's not a uniformed soul in sight.
No conscripts here; just an army of the hungry
queuing for their rations.

Outside it's snowing harder.
Inside, the radio plays.
Is that Glenn Miller Band?
Am I hearing *In the Mood?*

Lisa Rossetti

Mental Health

Bitter Wind

It's hard to keep warm today.
A bitter wind blows through the land.
I fear for these vulnerable people

who share their stories with me,
all their years of just about coping,
lost opportunities, lost relationships.

My mother never had property or savings, he said.
Nothing but a hard life and an unhappy marriage.
My father was a violent man.

I spent twenty years caring for her;
but our last words were not good.
I still feel guilty, waking at night.

I was damaged as a child. He falls silent.
I say, *You are a brave man – a survivor.*
He takes my hand. We sit together.

Winter is the worst of times
for people living precarious lives;
and damage is still being done.

Lisa Rossetti

Film With No Star

In the movie of my life,
I am absent on set.

No one has seen me for days.
My trailer is empty.

I absconded some time ago,
unhappy with the direction.

For it is all a fiction.
This script. This ideology.

This film with no star.

Cath Davies

Sand Dog

He's there again,
back propped against
the old church wall,
dressed in army khakis,
his surviving camouflage.

His faithful dog sleeps by his side;
a golden Labrador, head upon its paws.
But look closer. The dog is made of sand,
cleverly sculpted each day he's on the streets.

Are they for real, this dog or man? They try to tell us it's a scam.
Anyone can buy a uniform on E-bay, or the outdoor shop.

One thing's for sure, no passer-by has yet
spat at you, or stoved in the dog's head.

Lisa Rossetti

How Jimmy* Died

Jimmy died
with his fingers crossed.

So scared was he
of going to the other place.

*Jimmy Savile

Cath Davies

Shit Into Compost

I tell you, hypothyroidism is truly shit.
My doctors were in denial; they would not help me.
Exhausted, I barely managed to struggle through my days.

Every day I drank a murky toxic brew
of Shame, Struggle and Anger.
Blighting my life with hopelessness and depression.

Depression is a lonely guesthouse.
Have you been there?
Nobody could save me

from the ragged visitors
of regrets and reproaches,
shuffling through my mind.

I tell you truly that it was writing that saved me:
my Journal, my poetry, my storytelling and later my art.
These are the alchemies that transformed my Shit into Compost.

And from this, I have grown vibrant and flourishing
watering the roots of my Tree of Life with new Hope.
And I am grown green with Creativity and leafy with Promise.

Forget making lemonade out of the lemons that Life hands you!
Be bolder, cruder, more fucking personal.

Write about your Shit, all of it.

And then turn it into Compost.

Lisa Rossetti

Climate

Warming Woman

I am warming woman;
my agency
a wildfire in Australia.

I dispense hurricanes to America,
and breathe
the lungs of billions.

I fill space;
melt icecaps into tears;
let coral reefs fall through my fingers.

For I am earthed,
my volatility
birthing this world of chaos.

Cath Davies

Listening to the Grasslands

The Spirit of the Grasslands lives within me.
It knows that I can be free.
The Grasslands know I can live simply
on the earth, and feel that I belong.

The roots go down deep,
a whole system working together, replenishing.
Providing shelter for the small things, nourishing,
allowing quiet dark waters to run through.

The Grasslands in me know many things to tell me.
They whisper quietly. So I must be still –
and even stiller to hear - curious, looking, listening.
No raucousness, no forcing of the way.

I can tread a path already trod,
or be the pioneer with Freedom to roam.
How easily the grass parts –
how gently I can make my path.

The Grasslands in me know
that I too need this interconnection,
this joyful noticing of the small things:
leaf, berry, bird, flower.

They know my need for safety and for space.
The landscape is open before me.
It holds secrets, each thing feeding another,
connected in ways that support life.
The Grasslands listen to me - and I listen to them.

Lisa Rossetti

Wildfire

I walk down the road.
At the first junction, turn left.

All is normal. The sun is high
and the trees are green
but for the grass, yellow and scorched.

It is only at the end of the side road,
something is amiss.

A fence is black and burned.
The trees stand black in awkward shapes.
A garden is wasteland.

It is like a hole in the world
has burnt through all our certainty.

And I ask myself where I am?
India? Australia?

No, this is my home.
A cold country
in the Northern hemisphere.

Cath Davies

Climate Conference

We are posing questions
in a high-ceilinged room with
long windows, blinds drawn.

Our urgent cadences
keep on falling
into still warm air.

Murmurings circulate
between us as
insistent as dying bees,

or perhaps small birds
fallen from the nest
before they fledged.

The talk here is
of suppressing voices,
loss of trust.

We anticipate their fear
and battles, focusing
on deals and compromise.

Outside a dog barks in urgent staccato.
The trees are waving their
messages to us back and forth

in verdant semaphore.
They tremble as they
lean to catch the breeze.

Lisa Rossetti

Generation Zero

In the drama of climate change,
there is no protagonist. No villain.

No triumph of good over evil.
No story arc. No lesson learnt.

Instead, a slow awakening.
A chance for heroes, yes.

But most of all, a generation zero,
of all ages, inching to the precipice.

Cath Davies

Compartments

In the commuter train
we sit in rows,
in hushed contemplation
of our cellular phones.

Outside, the countryside,
rounded by weather, eroded by time,
is flashing by the windows invisibly,
blurred by ravenous speed.

We do not notice
the chronology written
in ancient tracks, ridges,
furrows and mounds.

Six birds fly up unseen
out of a rough wheatfield,
its boundaries thick
with ruffled foliage.

Our bodies swaying, we snake
through our fragile topography.
Our thoughts engrossed with oracles,
their stories shifting like sand.

Lisa Rossetti

History and Place

Chester's Child Soldiers

You see them every day, long lines of small children
recruited to the Roman army, clutching their yellow plastic shields;
enacting the bloody occupation from which this city rose.

Pale faced Britanni, with skinny legs and fair hair tousled
by the wind gusting up from the rebuilt amphitheatre floor.
They clutch at their mock armour, hi-viz jackets flapping.

Leather sandals slap upon the stones and gravel.
Giggling, the child soldiers march in twos over the bridge.
The centurion roars out his commands: Sin, Dex, Sin, Dex!

He's a brute of a man, this grim-faced Roman,
thick thighs tanned by wind and sun, chest encased
in its heavy carapace of military might and muscle.

'Child exploitation by the Oppressors?' I say to their teacher.
She glares at me. She prefers to celebrate the myth
Of glorious war, our Roman history – and all they did to us.

Lisa Rossetti

The Birds Can Read

The birds can read.
For on Bastille Day in Caux,
they sing in the trees
opposite the Mayor's office.

On its stone walls,
inbetween the flags,
three words.
Liberte. Egalite. Fraternite.

I swear I heard them.

Cath Davies

Liverpool One

I walk through driving rain.
Deserted city.

Leaves as fallout,
the Pandemic years wear hard
on the skin.

A softer wind
is the music of the Mersey.

My hand falls from yours.
But the docks
still rise, still rise.

Cath Davies

Minerva's Shrine

To erase a woman completely takes Time.
I have waited centuries in my niche, gazing over this Cestrian field.
Once it was a mass of men and muscle, quarrying stone.
They carved me, called me out of this sandstone rock.
They laid flowers and libations at my feet.
Now all I see before me are rank weeds and cans.

Men praised me for my wisdom, for my love of poetry,
for my skills in medicine and practice of the arts.
Yet in all honesty the bridge builders were more entranced
by my other powers – commerce and strategy –
as they planned the river's span, the building of this Diva,
their walled city, fort and bridge.

Then came men with stony faces and hammers,
Zealots with a strange religion of a nailed God.
They came to obliterate all traces of Female Power.
Yet their hands were stayed by the merciful Gods,
by the traces of my long cloak. For they believed
I was someone else, their pure Virgin Goddess.

Here I stand, still trapped in stone,
my once smooth and lustrous face
now pockmarked and weather beaten.
My little owl is almost disappeared.
Yet in the approaching darkness
I feel his small feathered heart beat next to mine.

Lisa Rossetti

Affirmation and Hope

Life Calls

4th June, 2017 – the morning after the Manchester Bombing

Did I sleep? It is early.

The world awakens, as it always has,
rapturous birdsong pulsing, rising, calling.

In the street below, last night's revellers
come home, calling noisily to their friends.

The yellow rose still nods
on my neighbour's wall.

My breath comes to me as it always has,
silently pulsing, rising, calling.

My little cat comes to me for kindness;
I sooth her with my hands.

I won't go back to sleep – the sky is on fire.

Lisa Rossetti

Tight in the Bud

But all is to be dared –
because even a person of poverty feels the fire,
the ache, the yearning.
Though it be buried many long years
under a heavy snow
in the bleakest of black forests.
A hard rain falls on us,
numbing all longing,
yet that ember still glows
in any human heart,
rich or poor.
A small spark of Hope
tight in the bud
longs for its own flowering,
for fulfilment, for grace,
for consummation, for absolution,
for the birthright of Joy.
Even if we do not recollect
the promise we made
to ourselves at birth,
being lowly or exalted
in the eyes of the world.
Even if we are persuaded
to call this desire by other names,
by those who would keep us
dumb and dissatisfied.

Lisa Rossetti

Redemption Rain

We were all washed clean last night.
All of us washed clean by a miracle rain
that came quietly in the night,
bathing the planet in Redemption.
The whole world shining
bright as a handful of silver,
clean as forgiveness and hope.
The morning sunlight illuminates
the scribbled hieroglyphs of branches.
Now in Delaware,
the pilot rolls over in his bed.
Smelling coffee he leaves his boots by the chair,
ignoring the call from bomber base.
He pads instead through the soft rain
on bare feet
to the poolside,
where his children sit watching the dimpled water.
In Kobane the black and white flag
lies damply crumpled
on the floor of the truck.
The Brothers go shopping for figs and flat bread,
smiling at the market woman,
whose heads in bright scarves
bend quietly over glistening pomegranates.
In the Ukraine,
old men are climbing out of cellars,
breathing in the smell of wet earth and green fields.
They greet the young soldier boys,
who are already forgetting
to pick up their guns,

finding it easier to wave, thumbs up,
as the rain continues to fall softly upon
their shaven heads.
By the wall,
Jacob lays down his heavy jacket,
removes his helmet,
stretches his arms through
the gaping hole in the wall.
Stretching through the fine wet curtain of rain
towards the greening pastures
and small white goats,
he touches a small hand.
We were all washed clean last night.
All of us washed clean by the rain.
Today we are scanning the horizon
for rain clouds again.

Lisa Rossetti

The Wrong Number

She dialled up 2022.

It rang for ages, then went to options.

Option 1:
for war.

Option 2:
for the cost of living.

Option 3:
for the climate.

Option 4:
for hope no matter what.

To hear these options again please press 5.

She pressed 4.

Cath Davies

We Stand for Life

We stand for Life.
The gritty strength of ancient stone,
buried deep, excavated.
Its glittering mica traces on our fingers;
touch and connect.

We stand for Life.
Fingers dipped into cool water
anointing our foreheads.
Water is our common need,
refreshes our roots.

We stand for Life.
Crushing the herb leaf,
releasing fresh pungency,
for medicine and healing.
Green sap is common blood.

We stand for Life.
The ringing bowl vibrates.
Metal from the deep earth,
forged and hammered,
serving our rites.

We stand for Life.
The dry earth crumbles
around tangled dormant roots.
Our growth is entwined.

We stand for Life.
Fiercely or gently:
gently or fiercely.
Our deep connections.

Lisa Rossetti

Basic Rules for Night-time Spellcasting

A witch has come to your house.
She hides in your curtains.
She hangs motionless watching you.
She has no head,
just a long purple cloak.

Sometime the cloak flaps,
twisting towards you.

Outside in the twilight world
gas lamps flare greenish-white.
You hear once again
those invisible strangers
passing by your window.

Make a magic for the night.
Begin.

Reach out your hand
to the wall by your bed.
Touch the surface.
Feel how it is cool and solid.
This is fundamental.

Count the nine purple flowers
twining in the wallpaper garden.
Counting begins the magic.
Then stare into the picture on the wall
till it opens up, becomes a portal.
There are people moving in the painted snow.

You may travel with them
down the painted street.

Now you are gone into another land.
quite out of reach.

Till morning light seeps through again
illuminating the edges of the window,
bringing the promise of blue sky
restoring all the shapes
and colours of your room

Blessing you.
Banishing the witch.

Lisa Rossetti

Sashiko for the Soul

I am untangling the frayed edges of myself.
The ripped fabric of me is threadbare in places.
Worries and regret have worn away the stitching
that holds my garment together.

Here's a cobbled darn constructed with hasty clumsy stitches,
my yarn stabbed and yanked through the cloth impatiently.
It must all be undone.
All my mistakes must be unpicked.

I am peeling back the tattered scraps and uneven patching,
revealing the symbolic patterns hidden beneath.
These cyphers of protection of the hopeful future
I had once promised myself.

Then carefully, in the clear full light of day
I examine all the filaments that bind me to my past.
This one is weakened with shame;
that one succumbed to cruel moth.

So with my shining needle I now begin the process of restoration:
to thread back Hope into my fabric once more.

Lisa Rossetti

Note: Sashiko (literally "little stabs") is a Japanese form of decorative reinforcement stitching. Traditional sashiko was used to reinforce points of wear, or to repair worn places or tears with patches.

Sentences

Today, whatever sentience,
guile or talent I once had was superseded
by an AI.

I plan to relax by the pool
on my guaranteed universal income.

The weather will be warm,
and I will smile fondly and ironically
at my former efforts.

It's a tough gig, this century.
I miss the '80s.
But I will hold on to everything human.

Hope. Frailty. Fallibility.

You in your designer swimwear.

Cath Davies

Young Hearts

We were undestined, my generation,
to bring the peace and heal the planet.

We will have to trust them,
the young people I mean.

They will have to sort this out, this mess of our own making.
They are out there, all around us.

Socially aware, concerned with fairness, age-blind even.
They work hard with all of this load,

the awful acts, hatred, betrayals.
I know some don't seem to give a damn.

Still, we must trust them too.
Their young hearts ringing like bells.

Lisa Rossetti

Acknowledgements

'Letter To A Nuclear World', 'Wildfire', 'The Wrong Number' and 'Remembering The Poem' all published in 'Full Circle', the 2023 anthology celebrating Chester Poets' 50th anniversary. Many thanks to all at the group for this opportunity to be included and congratulations on such a milestone.

Many thanks to Marc Peter Spacey and all at Colwyn Bay Writers' Circle for ongoing support and inspiration every week to write for the group.

And thanks to Darrell, my husband and my parents, Paul and Sally, and all my friends, in person and online, who continue to give encouragement and support for my writing.

Cath

Poems published in online blogs and magazines include, 'Global Sacrifice' published in 'Blaze' in 2017; 'Grenfell Tower' in 'Militant Thistle' in 2018; 'Roof Times' published in 'International' in 2019, and 'Basic Rules' in 'The Lake', September 2023 edition.

'Sashiko for the Soul' Highly Commended by King Lear Prizes in 2023.

Many thanks to Mary Reynolds Thompson (author of A Wild Soul Woman) for her inspiration and encouragement in her Wild Scribe sessions. Also to Alison Smith (Founder of Women's School of Metamorphosis) for support, challenge and inspiration in her Poetry Garden sessions.

Also gratitude and thanks to my friends at Lapidus International for all your belief in my creativity. And of course, to my husband.

Lisa

About the Authors

Cath lives in Holywell, north Wales with her husband Darrell and dog Kato, and has been writing all her life. She has a 20-year work history in social care and currently works as a domestic assistant for ClwydAlyn housing association. She is also a founder member of Colwyn Bay Writers' Circle and has self-published several books of her poetry and short fiction, all with Amazon. She has been published online with literary e-zines Ink, Sweat & Tears, Nine Muses, Dear Reader and Dark Poets Club, and in 2020 was highly commended in the Disability Arts Cymru Outdoors/ Indoors Creative Word Award with her poem about the pandemic, 'A Nursery Rhyme'. She is passionate about writing about current events and the tremendous challenges we all face, and links to her books can be accessed at her WordPress site, www.cathdavies.com.

Lisa lives near the river in Chester with her husband and delightful cat. She is a storyteller, creative writer and a credentialled poetry therapy practitioner (International Federation of BiblioPoetry Therapy). She works mostly in the community with vulnerable people. Lisa is a local Wildlife Champion with Chester Zoo and founder of a community growing groups reclaiming unused urban spaces. She believes deeply in the power of Community to make the vital changes we need. Her poetry has been published in Ink, Sweat & Tears, The Lake, International Times, The Recusant, Blaze Blog, Brevis and various poetry pamphlets. Her other claim to fame is that one of her short stories was shortlisted for the Bridport Prize (2012). You can also find her on Facebook at www.facebook.com/TheStoryCafe.

Printed in Great Britain
by Amazon